# AFTER GOD'S OWN HEART

## The Life of King David

### Brian Johnston

Published by:

**HAYES PRESS Publisher**, Resources & Media,

The Barn, Flaxlands,

Royal Wootton Bassett,

Swindon, SN4 8DY,

United Kingdom

I0201503

# Table of Contents

# ABOUT THIS BOOK

———

These days, image is everything. The political candidate had better be blessed with confidence, charm and good looks. Forget his or her views on the real issues, it's the photogenic smile that counts ... Society has an obsession with celebrities who employ their own 'image consultants' ... Any positive endorsement in the world of advertising demands someone with fabulous looks ... someone who's the epitome of 'cool'.

What's happening? Society has become very superficial. We've forgotten that beauty is only skin deep. But wait a minute, the Bible says: '... *the LORD looks at the heart.*' To what extent are you influenced by the type of car she drives or the designer clothes he wears – the 'cool' manner, the flattering charms, the prestigious qualifications, career projections and net worth? Let international Bible teacher and radio broadcaster, Brian Johnston, help you check out what really counts with God.

# CHAPTER 1 - GOD LOOKS AT THE HEART

———

These days, image is everything. The political candidate had better be well blessed with confidence, charm and good looks. Forget his or her views on the real issues it's the photogenic smile that counts – together with being savvy with the media. Our society has an obsession with celebrities. Sports' 'superstars' like footballer David Beckham have their own 'image consultants'. A new kind of industry has been born. Their task is to project their client as a world icon. Nowadays any positive endorsement in the world of advertising demands someone with fabulous looks: someone who's the epitome of 'cool'. The advertisers' message is: if you want to be thought of as sophisticated, somebody to be admired, then you must have our product and then the image projected in the advert will materialize.

These strategies work. They're enormously successful because our society has become very superficial. We've forgotten that beauty is only skin deep. We've fooled ourselves into thinking that God is just as easily impressed as society around us. After all, we can always dress up our CV and spin a good story about our failures. But wait a minute ... The Bible tells us in the First Book of Samuel that the first king of Israel was a man called Saul. He cut a fine figure. He seemed the ideal role model –

tall, handsome and impressive. He was a head taller than all the others (1 Samuel 10:23). There was no-one like him along all the people (v.24).

Unfortunately, after making a good start, he proved to be foolish and disobedient. The 'people's man' turned out to be a disaster for them. In choosing Saul's replacement, the Bible tells us that God made a point of demonstrating his total rejection of this world's standards.

> "The LORD said to Samuel, "How long will you mourn for Saul, since I have rejected him as king over Israel? Fill your horn with oil and be on your way; I am sending you to Jesse of Bethlehem. I have chosen one of his sons to be king" ... You are to anoint for me the one I indicate." Samuel did what the LORD said. When he arrived at Bethlehem, the elders of the town trembled when they met him. They asked, "Do you come in peace?" Samuel replied, "Yes, in peace; I have come to sacrifice to the LORD. Consecrate yourselves and come to the sacrifice with me." Then he consecrated Jesse and his sons and invited them to the sacrifice. When they arrived, Samuel saw Eliab and thought, "Surely the LORD'S anointed stands here before the LORD." But the LORD said to Samuel, 'Do not consider his appearance or his height, for I have rejected him. The LORD does not look at the things man looks at. Man looks at the outward appearance, but the LORD looks at the heart."

*Then Jesse called Abinadab and made him pass in front*
*of Samuel. But Samuel said, "The LORD has not*
*chosen this one either." Jesse then made Shammah pass*
*by, but Samuel said, "Nor has the LORD chosen this*
*one." Jesse made seven of his sons pass before Samuel,*
*but Samuel said to him, "The LORD has not chosen*
*these." So he asked Jesse, "Are these all the sons you have?"*
*"There is still the youngest," Jesse answered, "but he is*
*tending the sheep." Samuel said, "Send for him; we will*
*not sit down until he arrives." So he sent and had him*
*brought in. He was ruddy, with a fine appearance and*
*handsome features. Then the LORD said, "Rise and*
*anoint him; he is the one." So Samuel took the horn*
*of oil and anointed him in the presence of his brothers,*
*and from that day on the Spirit of the LORD came*
*upon David in power. Samuel then went to Ramah"* (1
Samuel 16:1-13).

The key statement in all that we've read is this: 'Man looks at the
outward appearance, but the LORD looks at the heart.' Think
about it. What sort of 'outward things' do you look for in
people? Perhaps they're just the kind of things our culture
reinforces in all the ways we were thinking about to start with in
this chapter. To what extent are we influenced by the type of car
she drives or the designer clothes he wears – the 'cool' manner,
the flattering charms, the prestigious qualifications, career
projections and net financial worth? For some people first
impressions are lasting impressions and they're not based on very
much.

Have you ever wondered why God had Samuel look at each of Jesse's sons before revealing to Samuel that he had in fact chosen David? It's so hard for us not to be impressed by 'outward things', by mere externals. Surely God wanted to really emphasize the point to Samuel time and time again that externals don't count – it's what inside counts. God valued the 'inner qualities' he found in David, though he was the youngest son, and apparently overlooked initially even by his own father. That brings us to the question of what specific 'inner qualities' God values – and how we can develop that kind of character. We can find such a list in Colossians 3:12-14:

> *"Put on tender mercies, kindness, humility, meekness, longsuffering; bearing with one another, and forgiving one another, if anyone has a complaint against another, even as Christ forgave you, so you also must do. But above all these things put on love, which is the bond of perfection."*

These are qualities we're told to 'put on'. I find that tremendously encouraging. This isn't a question – certainly isn't to remain a question – of you've either got it or you haven't. We can clothe ourselves with – or sink down into – these things, we can acquire them in ever greater measure. So let's make sure we're taking time to pray for the development of these inner qualities in our lives and character. These are Christian qualities. They were found in all their perfection in the life of Jesus Christ. The apostle Paul was talking to believers on the Lord Jesus when he wrote these words. God's plan for Christ's followers is that we become more like Christ, the one we follow. All the inner qualities God values were modeled in Christ. God the Father declared from heaven: *'This is My beloved Son in whom I am well pleased'.*

Our lives, too, will please God when they become more like Christ's. It's the work of God's Spirit within us to bring about this change. That's the great possibility open to anyone who's experienced the new birth – which is the inner change that takes place when we place our faith in Jesus Christ, God's Son – the change only God can make in us so that we're fit for heaven. For the rest of our life as Christians we're to aim to become in daily life before others what we are already in God's sight. The old worldly perspective is to pass away. Paul says: *"From now on we regard no-one from a worldly point of view. Though we once regarded Christ in this way, we do so no longer"* (2 Corinthians 5:16).

These words tell us that a believer's view of Christ should be radically different from an unbeliever's and the believer's view of all men and women should now take its bearings from his or her view of Christ. Let's make sure we're not regarding anyone from a worldly point of view, obsessed with mere outward appearance. Let's take our bearings from our view of Christ, and look for the inner qualities that made his life the most attractive life ever lived on this planet. Let's aim to develop these qualities in ourselves first, and then encourage them in others around us.

# CHAPTER 2 - THE BATTLE IS THE LORD'S

———

When were you last faced with a challenge that was seemingly beyond your own abilities? How did you respond? One of the myths of our culture is the saying 'if you set your mind to it, you can do anything'. The Bible confronts that myth head-on in the famous story of David and Goliath which we come to in this chapter. Before we focus on David, I want you to read what the Bible had to say about all the Israelite soldiers in King Saul's army. We'll pick up the story as David sets out to join them.

> "Early in the morning David left the flock with a shepherd, loaded up and set out, as Jesse had directed. He reached the camp as the army was going to its battle positions, shouting the war cry. Israel and the Philistines were drawing up their lines facing each other. David left his things with the keeper of supplies ran to the battle lines and greeted his brothers. As he was talking with them, Goliath, the Philistine champion from Gath, stepped out from his lines and shouted his usual defiance and David heard it. When the Israelites saw the man, they all ran from him in great fear" (1 Samuel 17:20-24).

So that's how they responded when faced with overwhelming odds. And who would blame them for running away? No matter how they tried to set their mind on the fabulous reward the king offered, they just couldn't bring themselves to go solo against Goliath the giant. But in the same place where the Bible explodes the myth that tells us we can do anything we set our mind to – in the same place, it demonstrates for us that we can do anything in God's strength. It's David that shows us this when:

> *"He took his staff in his hand, chose five smooth stones from the stream, put them in the pouch of his shepherd's bag and with his sling in his hand, approached the Philistine. Meanwhile the Philistine with his shield-bearer in front of him kept coming closer to David. He looked David over and saw that he was only a boy, ruddy and handsome, and he despised him. He said to David, "Am I a dog that you come at me with sticks?" And the Philistine cursed David by his gods. "Come here," he said, "and I'll give your flesh to the birds of the air and the beasts of the field!"*

> *David said to the Philistine, "You come against me with sword and spear and javelin, but I come against you in the name of the LORD Almighty, the God of the armies of Israel, whom you have defied. This day the LORD will hand you over to me, and I'll strike you down and cut off your head. Today I will give the carcasses of the Philistine army to the birds of the air and the beasts of the earth, and the whole world will know that there is a God in Israel. All those gathered here will know that*

*it is not by sword or spear that the LORD saves; for the battle is the LORD's, and he will give all of you into our hands."*

*As the Philistine moved closer to attack him, David ran quickly towards the battle line to meet him. Reaching into his bag and taking out a stone, he slung it and struck the Philistine on the forehead. The stone sank into his forehead, and he fell face down on the ground. So David triumphed over the Philistine with a sling and a stone; without a sword in his hand he struck down the Philistine and killed him. David ran and stood over him. He took hold of the Philistine's sword and drew it from the scabbard. After he killed him, he cut off his head with the sword. When the Philistines saw that their hero was dead, they turned and ran"* (1 Samuel 17:40-51).

So now it was the enemy's turn to run away. Every day, every Christian has an enemy to face. He's as real as Goliath was, and much more intimidating. Our wrestling, the Bible tells us, is not against flesh and blood (Ephesians 6:12). It's a spiritual conflict. The forces that oppose us are headed up by God's Adversary, the Devil. He's no less real just because we can't see him. But if we resist him, through the Bible, God promises us that the Devil will flee from us (James 4:7). But to resist him we need to first draw near to God – need to avail ourselves of the armor, the protection and strength that God provides (Ephesians 6).

We're no match for him in our own strength – just as the Israelites were no match for Goliath in their own strength. But by God's help we can exercise faith overcoming the doubts the Devil sows, we can be known for our truthfulness and by it oppose Satan's lies, and we can practice righteous living defying any tendency to be devious, always being ready to share God's good news, and to put our knowledge of Scripture to good use – not forgetting that it's all by prayer and by the Holy Spirit in us that we can live victoriously. Check out those defensive strategies from Ephesians chapter 6 - they all relate to the armor itemized there. The Israelites in Saul's army had forgotten God's promises which he'd made to them way back in Deuteronomy chapter 20:

> *"When you go to war against your enemies and see horses and chariots and an army greater than yours, do not be afraid of them, because the LORD your God, who brought you up out of Egypt, will be with you. When you are about to go into battle, the priest shall come forward and address the army. He shall say: "Hear, O Israel, today you are going into battle against your enemies. Do not be faint-hearted or afraid; do not be terrified or give way to panic before them. For the LORD your God is the one who goes with you to fight for you against your enemies to give you victory"* (Deuteronomy 20:1-4 NIV).

The reason Israelite armies were never to be afraid as they entered into battle lay in the assurance that their God was going with them to fight for them. The battle was the Lord's. The victory was his too. But by the time of Saul, the only person in

Israel to claim that promise was David, the young shepherd boy. David's victory that day was not the result of youthful bravado. Far from it. We were thinking last time of the inner qualities in David which God so appreciated. Here's one of them. David's uncomplicated way of taking God at his Word, and truly believing the promises God makes. David wasn't going into battle in his own strength. We can see he really claimed this 500-year-old promise, because he said to Goliath: *'I come against you in the name of the LORD Almighty ... for the battle is the LORD's'.*

In other words David was using the principle that the prophet would later express as; *'Not by might nor by power, but by my Spirit, says the LORD Almighty'* (Zechariah 4:6). But what about us? Think again about those words of Deuteronomy 20:3 (NASB): *'You are approaching the battle against your enemies today.'* Yes, today our Adversary will be prowling around us as a roaring lion seeking to devour someone (1 Peter 5:8). Perhaps that unrelenting spiritual battle is being intensified by some impending crisis? Or maybe some showdown is looming? Fears are about to be confronted. We each may be facing different 'Goliaths' – at work, at home or in our personal lives, *'Do not be afraid ... your God ... goes with you, to fight for you against your enemies'* (Deuteronomy 20:3,4).

In the battles of life, we may take on responsibilities for which, in measure, we, or others, feel we're qualified. But that doesn't remove the need for faith; nor does faith remove the need for God-given qualifications. Didn't David speak of how he was qualified to face the giant due to his experience in dealing with wild animals while defending his father's sheep? But qualified as he was, it was still in faith that he had to go out. His victory still had to come from God in the first place. Go into today's battle armed with the great Bible promises which are still just as relevant for you. Like Paul we can say: *"I can do all things through Him who strengthens me"* (Philippians 4:13). And what of that wonderfully personal promise in Hebrews chapter 13 verse 5? 'He himself has said, *"I will never desert you, nor will I ever forsake you"*'.

# CHAPTER 3 - TRUE FRIENDSHIP

———

What qualities do you appreciate most in a friend? David, whose life we're looking at, had a really close friend, Jonathan. David, of course, was brought to Jonathan's attention as a result of his heroic victory over Goliath. Fresh from his triumph, David went straight into a debriefing session with the king, and then we read in First Samuel chapter 18:

> *"After David had finished talking with Saul, Jonathan became one in spirit with David, and he loved him as himself ... And Jonathan made a covenant with David because he loved him as himself. Jonathan took off the robe he was wearing and gave it to David, along with his tunic, and even his sword, his bow and his belt"* (1 Samuel 18:1-4).

Perhaps it's unfair to make the contrast, because the circumstances were different, but David's acceptance of the gift of Jonathan's tunic contrasts with his rejection of Saul's tunic earlier. Perhaps you'll remember how before the contest with Goliath:

> *"Saul dressed David in his own tunic. He put a coat of armour on him and a bronze helmet on his head. David fastened on his sword over the tunic and tried walking*

*around, because he was not used to them. "I cannot go in
these," he said to Saul, 'Because I am not used to them."
So he took them off"* (1 Samuel 17:38-39).

On the other hand, maybe the contrast serves, in a way, to
symbolize how well David and Jonathan were matched as
soul-mates. The same could certainly never be said of David and
Saul. What's more, when Jonathan gave his tunic to David –
there was no question of expecting it back again. This was his
investment into the friendship, if you like. It's a simple point,
but so true, that if we're looking for true friendship, we're going
to have to invest something of ourselves in it. It'll hardly be
true friendship unless the contribution we make is an unselfish
one, and not a self-serving one. It's also significant that we read
of Jonathan making a covenant with David. This was a truly
committed friendship. Right from the start Jonathan was
signaling that he didn't anticipate falling in and out of friendship
in the way we often see children doing with each other – often
for what seems to us like trivial reasons.

One important aspect of commitment within a true Christian
friendship is the practice of holding each other accountable.
With a true friend we can commit to holding each other
accountable in serving the Lord. We come to value their
objective counsel, even correction at times when necessary. The
Bible proverb talks about the wounds of a friend being faithful
(Proverbs 27:6). That's this idea. A true friend is the best person
to give us the kind of straight talk we all need at times. We can
take it from them because of the quality of the relationship –
the quality of the friendship – between us. A true friend will not
always be uncritical of us. For many of us, of course, our marriage

partner is our best friend – and what a blessing when they carry out this role for us, and we do it for them. A couple of chapters later, in First Samuel 20, it's as if another window is opened to us showing us the depth of the friendship between David and Jonathan. I'm sure these are fully featured in the storyline so that they might also serve as a model for our friendship.

This episode takes place at a critical time for David. Saul has become insanely jealous of David. He's jealous of David's popularity and of his evident relationship with God who blesses him with success in all his duties. Saul's jealousy has already exploded more than once in murderous intent towards David. By chapter 20, David has had to go into hiding, away from the presence of Saul. It's now that he really begins to appreciate the confiding relationship he has with Jonathan, his true friend at the palace. As David tells Jonathan the extent to which he is in fear of losing his life, Jonathan at once replies: *'Whatever you say, I will do for you'* (v.4). Remember the prodigal son in the story Jesus told (Luke 15)?

As long as his money lasted, we can presume he had so-called friends. But when the money was gone, so were they. That's hardly friendship. It's been said that when you're in trouble you get to know who your true friends are. In David's time of crisis, Jonathan is there for him. A friend in need – and a friend indeed. David explains to Jonathan that he plans to test Saul's current attitude towards him by seeing what the king's reaction will be to David's planned absence from a celebratory meal. Jonathan agrees to bring David word by means of a coded message which he interprets in advance for David. Before they leave each other at this defining moment, we read that Jonathan says:

*"... show me unfailing kindness like that of the LORD as long as I live, so that I may not be killed, and do not ever cut off your kindness from my family – not even when the LORD has cut off every one of David's enemies from the face of the earth." So Jonathan made a covenant with the house of David, saying, "May the LORD call David's enemies to account." Jonathan made David reaffirm his oath out of love for him, because he loved him as he loved himself* (1 Samuel 20:14-17).

I suppose, sadly, there would be a tendency by some today to view this kind of language describing David and Jonathan's relationship as questionable, or by it jump to a wrong assumption. But the Bible is holding this friendship up as an example. The closeness of their friendship was totally honorable before God. We can be fully confident that there was absolutely nothing improper or impure about it. When Jonathan made David reaffirm his vow because of Jonathan's own love for him, it's telling us that Jonathan was motivated not by anything he could stand to gain – actually he stood to lose any succession rights to the throne he might once have thought he had. But he made David reaffirm his commitment to their friendship purely because of his own love. Quite selfless, wasn't it? So what happened? Well, we read on that:

*"David hid in the field, and when the New Moon festival came, the king sat down to eat. He sat in his customary place by the wall, opposite Jonathan, and Abner sat next to Saul, but David's place was empty ... Then Saul said to his son Jonathan, "Why hasn't*

*the son of Jesse come to the meal, either yesterday or today?" Jonathan answered, "David earnestly asked me for permission to go to Bethlehem ... Saul's anger flared up at Jonathan and he said to him, "You son of a perverse and rebellious woman! Don't I know that you have sided with the son of Jesse to your own shame and to the shame of the mother who bore you? As long as the son of Jesse lives on this earth, neither you nor your kingdom will be established. Now send and bring him to me, for he must die!"*

*"Why should he be put to death? What has he done?" Jonathan asked his father. But Saul hurled his spear at him to kill him. Then Jonathan knew that his father intended to kill David, Jonathan got up from the table in fierce anger, on that second day of the month he did not eat, because he was grieved at his father's shameful treatment of David"* (1 Samuel 20:17-34).

Jonathan put his friendship with David before any personal ambition of his own. Now that's true friendship of the highest quality. There has to be give and take in any friendship, and there's definitely plenty of giving on Jonathan's part here. Yes, friendship can be costly at times. It may cost us loss of face or our own reputation or someone else's favor when we defend a friend against baseless slander. But it'll be a cost worth paying. Jonathan knew that in David, he'd chosen for a friend someone who was going forward in his life with the Lord. Remember his words from earlier? 'When the LORD has cut off every one of David's enemies from the face of the earth'. Yes, this was the clear insight Jonathan had through their friendship. When we're looking for a companion with whom to enjoy true friendship, and to further our own walk with God, we can do no better than find a friend who's marked out as someone going forward in his or her life with the Lord. Then all those other qualities revealed in this model friendship will fall into place – like being committed, being confiding, and simply being there when we need them.

# CHAPTER 4 - A MATTER OF CONSCIENCE

———

How do you discover God's will in your life? Do you look to circumstances or to the advice of trusted friends or do you prayerfully consider the words of the Bible – or maybe a combination of all three? Since we're looking at the life of David, let's have a look and see how he found God's will in one of the decisions he had to make. Take the time when:

> *"Saul took three thousand chosen men from all Israel and set out to look for David and his men near the Crags of the Wild Goats. He came to the sheep pens along the way; a cave was there, and Saul went in to relieve himself. David and his men were far back in the cave. The men said, "This is the day the LORD spoke of when he said to you, 'I will give your enemy into your hands for you to deal with as you wish'"* (1 Samuel 24:2-4).

If we can just break into the story there - ask yourself what factors might have convinced David that it was God's will for him to kill Saul? Here was wonderful providence for a start! Surely, he might have thought, these circumstances have been arranged by God. Of all the caves in that region, Saul had chosen to come for a comfort break and a lie-down in the very cave in which David and his men were hiding! Talk about a golden opportunity for David! Added to that, there was the advice of his trusted companions. Their advice proclaimed this as a

God-given opportunity for David to be rid of the man who had made himself David's enemy. Circumstances, and the advice of friends, seem to be in full agreement. So what does David do?

> "David crept up unnoticed and cut off a corner of Saul's robe. Afterwards, David was conscience-stricken for having cut off a corner of his robe. He said to his men, "The LORD forbid that I should do such a thing to my master, the LORD's anointed, or lift my hand against him; for he is the anointed of the LORD." With these words David rebuked his men and did not allow them to attack Saul. And Saul left the cave and went his way" (1 Samuel 24:4-7).

Evidently, David didn't consider circumstances and advice to be totally reliable guides – at least not at this time. We're even told the additional factor that convinced David he shouldn't mistreat Saul in any way. It was David's conscience, as instructed by the Word of God. Saul had been anointed by the LORD as ruler over his inheritance (1 Samuel 10:1), and the Law of Moses (Exodus 22:28) had decreed that a ruler of the people was not even to be so much as cursed or spoken evil against. In fact, David's conscience was so tender, as he reflected further on this, that he was now ashamed he'd affronted Saul's dignity by simply having cut off a corner of his robe. I find that degree of sensitivity quite remarkable in a man of war, one whose own life has been threatened more than once by this same man whom he has spared.

How could David do that? One thing he appears to have done was to stop thinking of Saul as his enemy, the one who was standing between him and the throne which God had promised David. And to think of him instead as having God's anointing on him. That kind of mental adjustment is something we too need to make at times. When our plans are frustrated, it's easy to resent whoever is blocking us. But if the one who is being unjustifiably awkward is a brother or sister in Christ, then we need to remind ourselves that he or she is not an obstacle, but the brother or sister for whom Christ died.

Some of us may have grown up with the 'situation ethics' of the 1960s. Situation ethics argues that we may go against our conscience if it's for the sake of a supposedly greater good or if it's to achieve an outcome that's somehow considered to be 'more loving'. But it can never be right to go against our conscience when the conscience is informed by a clear biblical principle. Back in the story of David and Saul, we've now got to the point where David exits the cave behind Saul – to let him know what's happened.

> "Then David went out of the cave and called out to Saul, "My lord the king!" When Saul looked behind him, David bowed down and prostrated himself with his face to the ground. He said to Saul, "Why do you listen when men say, 'David is bent on harming you'? This day you have seen with your own eyes how the LORD gave you into my hands in the cave. Some urged me to kill you, but I spared you; I said, 'I will not lift my hand against my master, because he is the LORD's anointed'" (1 Samuel 24:8-10).

Notice how David summarizes his decision-making. He'd weighed up how God had given Saul into his hands; he'd listened to the arguments of those who urged him to kill Saul; but finally, what had overruled the decision was a consideration of the dignity of the office into which God had placed Saul – the honor of the LORD's anointing was on him, and God's Word taught him to respect that. Now David continues:

> *"... look at this piece of your robe in my hand! I cut off the corner of your robe but did not kill you. Now understand and recognize that I am not guilty of wrongdoing or rebellion. I have not wronged you, but you are hunting me down to take my life. May the LORD judge between you and me. And may the LORD avenge the wrongs you have done to me, but my hand will not touch you ... May the LORD be our judge and decide between us. May he consider my cause and uphold it; may he vindicate me by delivering me from your hand." When David finished saying this, Saul ... said "You have treated me well, but I have treated you badly. You have just now told me of the good you did to me; the LORD gave me into your hands, but you did not kill me. When a man finds his enemy, does he let him get away unharmed? May the LORD reward you well for the way you treated me today. I know that you will surely be king and that the kingdom of Israel will be established in your hands"* (1 Samuel 24:11-20).

Finally now, David's made all of his thinking clear. He's relying on God to judge his case and to avenge him of his enemies. He won't take matters into his own hands, but rather leave them in God's hands. God has promised David the throne, and David, for his part, is prepared to wait on the LORD's own timing to finally establish him as king. So David is restrained from avenging himself and from spoiling his character by doing so. That's the difference here between David making God's promise happen, and David allowing God to fulfill it in his own time. Once again, David's shown himself to be a man after God's own heart – shown himself to be a man like his greater Son, the Lord Jesus, about whom the apostle Peter says: *"When they hurled their insults at him, he did not retaliate; when he suffered, he made no threats. Instead, he entrusted himself to him who judges justly"* (1 Peter 2:23).

When it comes to our own decision-making, while it will always be wise to weigh up carefully our circumstances and the advice of others, what we must give full weight to is the example and attitude of Christ, and the clear guiding principles of God's Word, the Bible – all working through a conscience made sensitive through prayer in the Holy Spirit.

# CHAPTER 5 - SECURE IN THE LORD

---

S omeone once dumped a large load of rubbish on another man's private property. While looking through the mess, the man found the offender's name and address. He quickly loaded up the rubbish, drove to the person's house, and dumped the mess in his front yard. What would you have done? Are we ever justified in trying to 'get even' with someone? That's the issue we explore in the next episode of David's life. It comes at a time when:

> "David moved down into the Desert of Maon. A certain man in Maon, who had property there ... was very wealthy. He had a thousand goats and three thousand sheep, which he was shearing in Carmel. His name was Nabal and his wife's name was Abigail. She was an intelligent and beautiful woman, but her husband ... was surly and mean in his dealings. While David was in the desert, he heard that Nabal was shearing sheep. So he sent ten young men and said to them, "Go up to Nabal at Carmel and greet him in my name ... 'I hear that it is sheep-shearing time. When your shepherds were with us, we did not ill-treat them, and the whole time... nothing of theirs was missing. Ask your own servants and they will tell you. Therefore be favorable

*towards my young men, since we come at a festive time.*
*Please give your servants and your son David whatever*
*you can find for them."'*

*... Nabal answered David's servants, "Who is this*
*David? Who is this son of Jesse? Many servants are*
*breaking away from their masters these days. Why*
*should I take my bread and water, and the meat I have*
*slaughtered for my shearers, and give it to men coming*
*from who knows where?" David's men turned round*
*and ... reported every word"* (1 Samuel 25:1-12).

David felt he'd real cause to be offended by this response to his polite and reasonable request. Nabal acted as if he'd never heard of David. That's possible, I suppose, but I suggest it's unlikely. Even the Philistines (1 Samuel 21) had heard of David's fame. Anyway, even if Nabal had been sincere in this, and really did think it was prudent to be cautious, he could still have been respectful in his reply. David had been reduced to his present distress as a result of the good service he'd done his country, and here he was now being considered to be a bad person! It must have been hard to take. So *"David said to his men "Put on your swords!" So they put on their swords, and David put on his. About four hundred men went up with David, while two hundred stayed with the supplies"* (1 Samuel 25:13).

That might seem at first like an understandable reaction – after all we're accustomed to hearing about 'road rage' and a whole lot else. But wait a minute, Saul has already treated David much worse, and David has just spared his life! Where's your consistency, David? Well, we're not always consistent either.

Maybe David had grown to expect the worst from Saul, and he was prepared for it. But with Nabal he was surprised, he was caught off guard. Probably we've experienced something much the same. If we know we're going to be up against someone who's likely to be a bit awkward, we'll probably prepare specially for that eventuality and we'll work hard at being gracious. On the other hand, someone else may be having a bad day, and may say something hurtful to us, and because it's so unexpected, we're caught off guard, and maybe react in the heat of the moment. Meanwhile as David prepares to go the warpath, the story takes another twist:

> "One of the servants told Nabal's wife Abigail: "David sent messengers from the desert to give our master his greetings, but he hurled insults at them. Yet these men were very good to us. They did not ill-treat us, and the whole time we were out in the fields near them nothing was missing. Night and day they were a wall around us all the time we were herding our sheep near them. Now think it over and see what you can do, because disaster is hanging over our master and his whole household. He is such a wicked man that no-one can talk to him."

> Abigail lost no time. She took two hundred loaves of bread, two skins of wine, five dressed sheep, five seahs of roasted grain, a hundred cakes of raisins and two hundred cakes of pressed figs, and loaded them on donkeys. Then she told her servants, "Go on ahead; I'll follow you." But she did not tell her husband Nabal.

*As she came riding her donkey into a mountain ravine, there were David and his men descending towards her, and she met them ...*

*When Abigail saw David, she quickly got off her donkey and bowed down before David with her face to the ground. She fell at his feet and said: "My lord, let the blame be on me alone. Please let your servant speak to you; hear what your servant has to say. May my lord pay no attention to that wicked man Nabal. He is just like his name – his name is Fool, and folly goes with him. But as for me, your servant, I did not see the men my master sent. Now since the LORD has kept you, my master, from bloodshed and from avenging yourself with your own hands, as surely as the LORD lives and as you live, may your enemies and all who intend to harm my master be like Nabal. And let this gift, which your servant has brought to my master, be given to the men who follow you. Please forgive your servant's offence, for the LORD will certainly make a lasting dynasty for my master, because he fights the LORD's battles. Let no wrongdoing be found in you as long as you live ...*

*When the LORD has done for my master every good thing he promised concerning him and has appointed him leader over Israel, my master will not have on his conscience the staggering burden of needless bloodshed or of having avenged himself"* (1 Samuel 25:14-31).

It was quite a speech, wasn't it? Abigail proved again that wisdom is better than war. In her diplomacy, she prepared the very best. Not the bread, meat and water that David would have earlier settled for, but raisins, figs and wine. In stark contrast to her husband's rudeness, Abigail presented her case to David by showing great deference and respect. Very graciously, she was content to suffer blame for the fault of her husband. She excused his manner as folly, not malice. She pleaded she'd been ignorant of what had gone on, hinting perhaps that she could have influenced the situation had she known about it earlier.

But most remarkable of all, she showed her keen insight into the purposes the LORD had for David. What a contrast to her husband professing he never so much as knew of David's existence! And so she rested her case as one seeking now to defend David's honor. David, she foretold, would prosper over Saul one day, and how tragic it would be for David if he should have this blemish on his record – his good character spoiled because he'd once hastily avenged himself and in the process spilled innocent blood. Yes, it's hard for us not to sin when we're angry (Ephesians 4:26). So Abigail's defense all adds up to quite a formidable argument. And it was successful, for:

> *"David said to Abigail, "Praise be to the LORD, the God of Israel, who has sent you today to meet me. May you be blessed for your good judgment and for keeping me from bloodshed this day and from avenging myself with my own hands. Otherwise, as surely as the LORD, the God of Israel, lives, who has kept me from harming*

> *you, if you had not come quickly to meet me, not one*
> *male belonging to Nabal would have been left alive by*
> *daybreak"* (1 Samuel 25:32-34).

Perhaps you can think of someone who's recently mistreated you.
I hope God's Word will affect your attitude today. Shortly after
this incident, God struck Nabal and he died. That would seem to
illustrate the word of God directly to us through Paul in Romans
chapter 12 (v.19-21):

> *"Do not take revenge, my friends, but leave room for*
> *God's wrath, for it is written: "It is mine to avenge;*
> *I will repay," says the Lord. On the contrary: "If your*
> *enemy is hungry, feed him; if he is thirsty, give him*
> *something to drink. In doing this, you will heap burning*
> *coals on his head." Do not be overcome by evil, but*
> *overcome evil with good."*

May God help us to overcome evil with good, encouraged to do
so by having looked at the life of David.

# CHAPTER 6 - FINDING STRENGTH IN THE LORD

⎯⎯⎯

This episode in the life-story of David challenges us to try to imagine what must have been a heart-breaking time for David and his men. And it raises the issue of how we react when faced with an overwhelming problem. Here was the situation facing David:

> "David and his men reached Ziklag on the third day. Now the Amalekites had raided the Negev and Ziklag. They had attacked Ziklag and burned it, and had taken captive the women and all who were in it, both young and old. They killed none of them, but carried them off as they went on their way. When David and his men came to Ziklag, they found it destroyed by fire and their wives and sons and daughters taken captive. So David and his men wept aloud until they had no strength left to weep" (1 Samuel 30:1-4).

Desperate, wasn't it? How their hearts must have sunk when they saw the first tell-tale smoke billowing up from the direction of their city. We can imagine them racing towards the city with a deepening sense of alarm and shock. Surely it couldn't be true. But it was – their worst fears were realized. Everything precious to them was gone – either burned or removed. David had shared the same fate as his men: *"David's two wives had been captured –*

*Ahinoam of Jezreel and Abigail, the widow of Nabal of Carmel."*
Like the Christian in today's world, David wasn't immune to the
same kind of problems and pain as others around him.

What happened next is something we can all identify with.
When something goes wrong, we seem to need to find someone
to blame. It must be someone's fault. We might blame ourselves
or it might be someone near and dear to us. Sure it was the
criminals' fault, but who left the door unlocked, and why were
valuables left in full view? So David's men turned on him. They
blamed David for the loss of their wives and children. The record
is full of pathos when it tells us: *"David was greatly distressed
because the men were talking of stoning him; each one was bitter in
spirit because of his sons and daughters. But David found strength
in the LORD his God"* (1 Samuel 30:6).

How quickly David went from hero to zero in their estimation!
David himself could have questioned – indeed might well have
questioned – some of his decisions and actions that had led up
to this sorry state of affairs. But David lived in the present. He
knew there was only one place to turn to now, only one source of
help in this – and indeed in any – time of trouble (Psalm 46:1).
*'David found strength in the LORD his God.'* That's impressive.
This was no empty slogan or platitude. Here was a man whose
world was collapsing around him. But he strengthened himself
in God. How did he do that? In his life, David had a
well-developed habit of communion with God. The richness of
his prayer-life comes through to us in the many psalms he wrote
which find their place in our Bibles; prayers that are so real.

Time and again we come upon David in the psalms turning his problems over to God. In not a few of the psalms he begins by pouring out his heart to God, outlining his problem, confessing his need of God's help – but then he ends the same psalm by rejoicing in God his deliverer. He's worked through his problem with God in prayer. Prayer can be tremendously strengthening. When the apostle Paul was in prison at Rome he also knew this reality. Among the last words he wrote were these – addressed to Timothy:

> *"At my first defense no one supported me, but all deserted me; may it not be counted against them. But the Lord stood with me, and strengthened me, in order that through me the proclamation might be fully accomplished, and that all the Gentiles might hear; and I was delivered out of the lion's mouth" (2 Timothy 4:16-17).*

As we draw near to God in prayer, he's promised to draw near to us (James 4:7). That's a promise we can claim. David, too, having found strength in the Lord, went further to find more help from the Lord.

*"Then David said to Abiathar the priest, the son of Ahimelech, "Bring me the ephod." Abiathar brought it to him, and David enquired of the LORD, "Shall I pursue this raiding party? Will I overtake them?" "Pursue them," he answered. "You will certainly overtake them and succeed in the rescue" (1 Samuel 30:7,8).*

What a relief when we detect God's helpful answer after a time of crying out to him when we were in trouble! It'll usually involve us taking some corrective steps too. In David's case, he had to pursue his enemy.

> *"David and the six hundred men with him came to the Besor Ravine where some stayed behind, for two hundred men were too exhausted to cross the ravine. But David and four hundred men continued the pursuit ... and there the Amalekites were, scattered over the countryside, eating, drinking and reveling because of the great amount of plunder they had taken from the land of the Philistines and from Judah. David fought them from dusk until the evening of the next day, and ... David recovered everything the Amalekites had taken, including his two wives. Nothing was missing: young or old, boy or girl, plunder or anything else they had taken. David brought everything back. He took all the flocks and herds, and his men drove them ahead of the other livestock, saying, "This is David's plunder."*
>
> *Then David came to the two hundred men who had been too exhausted to follow him ... They came out to meet David and the people with him ... But all the evil men and troublemakers among David's followers said, "Because they did not go out with us, we will not share with them the plunder we recovered. However, each man may take his wife and children and go." David replied, "No, my brothers, you must not do that with what the LORD has given us. He has protected us and*

*handed over to us the forces that came against us ... The*
*share of the man who stayed with the supplies is to be the*
*same as that of him who went down to the battle. All*
*shall share alike"* (1 Samuel 30:9-24).

Do you know what was wrong with the logic of those men who
didn't want to share the spoils? They were thinking that they
had delivered themselves by their own strength and hard work.
David, who had personally committed the difficulty to the Lord,
now publicly acknowledges the help he's received. That's why
he can say: *"No, my brothers, you must not do that with what*
*the LORD has given us".* The Lord had given them help; the
Lord had given them the victory; and the Lord had given them
back their possessions. David had asked God for help, and now
he willingly recognized that God had given it. The spoil wasn't
theirs to withhold or dispose of how they pleased. Let's
remember to give God thanks for the help he gives us.

And David added: *'God has protected us and handed over to us*
*the forces that came against us.'* If God was able to do that, the
question arises as to why he ever allowed the problem to come
about in the first place. Perhaps it reminds us of the criticism of
some who grumbled against the Lord at the grave of Lazarus:

*"Could not this man, who opened the eyes of him who*
*was blind, have kept this man also from dying?" Jesus*
*therefore again being deeply moved within, came to the*
*tomb. Now it was a cave, and a stone was lying against*
*it. Jesus said: "Remove the stone." Martha, the sister of*
*the deceased, said to him, "Lord, by this time there will*

*be a stench, for he has been dead four days." Jesus said to*
*her, "Did I not say to you, if you believe, you will see the*
*glory of God?"* (John 11:37-40).

Of course, the Lord could have prevented Lazarus from dying at that time, but then there would have been no display of the glory of the Lord – and no deepening of Martha and Mary's faith, and what of those who came to faith as a result of that miracle worked on Lazarus? Not that we can always expect to understand why God allows bad things to come into our life. But David's experience can help us to have a realistic view of the difficulties we face at times. Our problems don't stop the moment we become Christians. We share in sufferings that are the common experience of humanity in a fallen world. Sometimes we bring suffering upon ourselves. At other times it may be a case of the Lord disciplining us or we face persecutions for the sake of our faith. God does not grant immunity to his children. What he does promise us is that he'll strengthen and help us through our difficulties.

We need to turn to him in crisis, and through prayer, strengthen ourselves in the Lord. If you're facing trouble just now, it doesn't need to end up in a hopeless mess, reflect on David's experience and let it bring you hope. In the final analysis, with the Lord's help, *'David recovered everything'.*

# CHAPTER 7 - GOD'S WRATH AND BLESSING

———

The Narnia Chronicles written by C.S. Lewis have fascinated children for generations, including my own. Usually without much help, children perceive the story for the allegory it is – with the lion Aslan corresponding to the Lord in the battle of good over evil. When one of the characters, Susan, discovers that the King is a lion and not a man, she asks: 'Is he – quite safe? I shall feel rather nervous about meeting a lion'. 'Safe?' the answer comes back, 'Who said anything about safe? 'Course he isn't safe. But he's good.'

It's a serious mistake, if in our Christianity, we think of God only as being like an indulgent Father providing for our needs while tolerating our disobedient behavior. The Bible not only tells us that God is a God of love, but it also reminds us that he's a consuming fire. It presents to us the goodness and severity of God. There's a misconception going around that somehow God has changed between the Old and New Testaments. But God never changes. In this installment from the life of David, we'll see how David discovered that God isn't safe, but is good.

> "David ... and all his men set out from Baalah of Judah to bring up from there the ark of God, which is called by the Name, the name of the LORD Almighty, who is enthroned between the cherubim that are on the ark. They set the ark of God on a new cart and brought

*it from the house of Abinadab, which was on the hill.*
*Uzzah and Ahio, sons of Abinadab were guiding the*
*new cart with the ark of God on it and Ahio was*
*walking in front of it. David and the whole house of*
*Israel were celebrating with all their might before the*
*LORD, with songs and with harps, lyres, tambourines,*
*sistrums and cymbals. When they came to the*
*threshing-floor of Nacon, Uzzah reached out and took*
*hold of the ark of God, because the oxen stumbled. The*
*LORD's anger burned against Uzzah because of his*
*irreverent act; therefore God struck him down and he*
*died there beside the ark of God"* (2 Samuel 6:1-7).

So the journey that day took them from Baale-judah which is
another name for Kiriath Jearim (see 1 Chronicles 13:6) all the
way to the threshing floor of Nacon or Chidon. A
threshing-floor in those times was usually land that was common
property situated at the centre of village life – often a rocky
outcrop with stones around the edge on some windy spot. From
April to June, the barley and wheat were harvested with a sickle.
The bundles of grain were then tied into sheaves, and loaded
on to donkeys or carts and taken to the threshing floor. There
the sheaves were spread out on the floor about a foot deep, and
threshing was done by beating them with a stick, or by driving
animals round, or by using a threshing sledge (which was a board
with bits or stone or iron fixed to it). By any one of these means
the stalks were chopped and the grain loosened, so the farmer
could then winnow. He did this by tossing the stalks in the air
with a wooden fork or shovel.

The straw was blown aside to be kept as winter feed for animals, but the more valuable and heavy grain fell back on the floor to be sifted and stored in earthenware jars or dry cisterns or barns. The Bible often uses the idea of threshing to symbolize God's judgement (e.g. Isaiah 23:23-29; Matthew 3:12). It's the Lord's work of threshing in our lives that separates between good and bad, between truth and error and between right and wrong. On this threshing floor God's judgment fell to show that something was wrong that day.

It happened when the ark of God arrived on the back of an oxen-pulled cart at the threshing floor of Nacon. It's possible, perhaps even probable, that Nacon wasn't the name of the man who owned the threshing floor. Because it (Nacon) means a stroke (as in a stroke of misfortune or disaster). Very likely this place was actually named after the disastrous incident we've been reading about – the time when Uzzah grabbed the ark of God and God struck him down dead on the spot with a single stroke.

We need to ask 'What's going on here? Why did this happen?' God's Law demanded that the ark of God – the sacred chest that contained the 2 stone tables of the Ten Commandments – should receive very particular treatment. It was associated with the presence of the holy God himself. So it couldn't be transported, far less handled, in just any old way. It had to be carried on poles on the shoulders of the priests or their assistants. David really should have known better. It was the kings' duty to read in the law of God every day. Maybe he'd been lulled into a false sense of security by the fact that when the enemy who had recently captured the ark had returned it to Israel, they'd put it on a new cart. It seemed like they'd got away with it. And perhaps David thought he could copy their 'new improved' way of doing things.

But it's not always right for us as Christians to copy the ways of non-Christians, or to go about serving God using new-fashioned modern ideas if they contradict things written in the Bible. This was far from being an unnecessary bit of 'small print' in the Law of God, and David's carelessness that day ended up costing Uzzah his life. But why Uzzah? Maybe there were other factors involved. The ark had been temporarily stored in the home of his parents. It's possible that familiarity had bred contempt, as the saying goes. I wonder if the holy ark had become just 'that wooden box in the corner'. Earlier in the life of David, we've had impressed on us the fact that God looks upon the heart – beyond the outward actions. Had Uzzah despised the ark in his heart that day?

Some Bible versions simply tell us that the oxen stumbled. And that may have been all that happened, leading Uzzah to put out his hand to steady the ark. But it's intriguing that it could be translated that the oxen 'shook' or that they 'discontinued' their journey – which might make us think of Balaam's donkey (Numbers 22). It tried to stop as Balaam drove it forward contrary to the word of the Lord. Perhaps Uzzah was intent on pushing the oxen forward too after they'd stopped. In any case, through Isaiah the prophet (66:2), God tells us that we should be the ones to shake or tremble at the Word of God, and discontinue any practice that God's Word opposes. David's emotional response was a mixture or anger and fear.

> *"David was angry because the LORD's wrath had*
> *broken out against Uzzah, and to this day that place*
> *is called Perez-Uzzah. David was afraid of the LORD*
> *that day and said, "How can the ark of the LORD ever*
> *come to me?" He was not willing to take the ark of the*
> *LORD to be with him in the City of David. Instead he*
> *took it aside to the house of Obed-edom the Gittite"* (2
> Samuel 6:8-10).

So David caused the journey to be aborted. David might be surprised, confused, displeased and disappointed – but two clear commands of God's Word had been broken. God had instructed in the days of Moses that not even the Levites were to touch the ark – it was to be carried by staves upon their shoulders. And while wagons could be used for transporting other tabernacle objects, they were not to be used for the most holy ark of God. David came to realize his mistake:

> *"The ark of the LORD remained in the house of*
> *Obed-edom the Gittite for three months, and the LORD*
> *blessed him and his entire household. Now King David*
> *was told, "The LORD has blessed the household of*
> *Obed-edom and everything he has, because of the ark of*
> *God." So David went down and brought up the ark of*
> *God from the house of Obed-edom to the City of David*
> *with rejoicing"* (2 Samuel 6:11,12).

After David saw that the Lord has blessed the home of Obed-edom. He renewed his efforts to bring the ark up to Jerusalem. He'd seen now the goodness as well as the severity of God. Learning from his mistake the first time round, he said:

*"No one is to carry the ark of God but the Levites; for the LORD chose them to carry the ark of God ... and to them he said ... you may bring up the ark of the LORD God of Israel, to the place that I have prepared for it. "Because you did not carry it at the first, the LORD our God made an outburst on us, for we did not seek Him according to the ordinance"* (1 Chronicles 15:1-28).

Let's make sure we learn this lesson from the life of David too. It's not for us to update the principles of God's Word either. In the New Testament we find clear principles for our church life that no modern reasoning has any right to update. In fact, we can be sure God will hold us accountable. He's signaled that through the record of this incident we've studied

# CHAPTER 8 - UNFULFILLED WISHES

━━━

Have you ever dreamt of doing great things for God? Accounts of the lives of Christian missionaries and visionaries often impress us. There's no shame in being ambitious for the Lord, or in having great spiritual desires. But have you ever thought you knew what God's will was, only to be surprised when later you came to a more careful knowledge of his will? I certainly have. Maybe some ministry you cherished hasn't prospered? Often what God actually requires of us is different from what we might imagine it to be. Our desires have to yield to his will. This sets the scene for our on-going look at the life of David:

> *"After the king was settled in his palace and the LORD had given him rest from all his enemies around him, he said to Nathan the prophet, "Here I am, living in a palace of cedar, while the ark of God remains in a tent." Nathan replied to the king, "Whatever you have in mind, go ahead and do it, for the LORD is with you"* (2 Samuel 7:1-3).

David was obviously thinking about building a house – a temple – for God. At that time, he'd brought the ark to Jerusalem, but this symbol of God's presence was just sitting in the tent David had pitched for it there. It seemed so incongruous to David that here he was living in a palace, while the ark of God was only in a tent. So David wanted to build a house for God, now that God had granted peace to him and his kingdom. David's desire seemed so right to Nathan. Many other men might have thought only about their own creature comforts. David could have put his feet up and enjoyed life in the palace. David's wish, instead, was focused on God, not himself. It was a spiritual desire, not a selfish one. Far from being distracted and forgetting about God, David wanted to honor God. So Nathan told him 'whatever you have in mind, go ahead and do it.' So off David went to do what was in his own mind. Surely this was one wish that was certain to be fulfilled.

> "But *that night the word of the LORD came to Nathan, saying: "Go and tell my servant David, 'This is what the LORD says: Are you the one to build me a house to dwell in? I have not dwelt in a house from the day I brought the Israelites up out of Egypt to this day. I have been moving from place to place with a tent as my dwelling. Wherever I have moved with all the Israelites, did I ever say to any of their rulers whom I commanded to shepherd my people Israel, "Why have you not built me a house of cedar?"'* (2 Samuel 7:4-7).

That was what David and Nathan had failed to reckon with. This wasn't something that God had asked for. David, it seems, with Nathan's encouragement initially, was up and running with a plan to build a temple according to all that 'was in his mind'. God, for whom the house was to be built, had neither asked for it nor specified his own choice of design. And David, of course, would need a design to build to. Presumably, he'd intended coming up with one of his own making if necessary since he was forging ahead with the project the prophet Nathan had already rubber-stamped. I'm absolutely convinced from all we know about David that what 'was in his mind' would have been the most splendid design David could conceive of.

But how many people down through the years have engaged in building projects that God never asked for? How many have built up a specialist church of one sort or another – a church specializing in one particular truth while overlooking others – and they sincerely felt it was God's will that they should add their own particular type of specialist church? There can be no doubting their sincerity. As with David, it seemed like the right thing to do. But the Lord's question remains the same: *'Did I ever say … why did you not build me [this]?'* That's the question that tests our desires. It's the searchlight by which our ambitions for God are examined. Is my desire fully consistent with all that God has asked me to do in his Word? For what God said through the prophet Isaiah, is true even in connection with the godliest men and women: *"For My thoughts are not your thoughts, neither are your ways My ways," declares the LORD"* (Isaiah 55:8).

But let's repeat: God was pleased with the sincerity of David's desire. He said: *"Because it was in your heart to build a temple for my Name, you did well to have this in your heart"* (1 Kings 8:18 NIV). David's desire had been appreciated, although he'd never be allowed to fulfill it. One reason why David wouldn't be allowed to design a house for God was because God had his own design! – written instructions which he gave (about 30 years later by some reckonings via David) to Solomon (1 Samuel 28:19, 20) whom God did ask to build his house or temple at Jerusalem.

Of course, God could have thanked David for his kind thought, and said: 'Fine, but I'll specify the design, not you.' I'm sure David would have had no problem with that. But there's another very basic reason why David couldn't build the temple for God – one which the Bible makes quite explicit. David was not chosen to build God's house because he was a man of war and had shed blood (1 Chronicles 28:3). But going back to our earlier assumption that David at first seemed to think he could just go off and build for God according to what was 'in his mind' – we might ask: 'How could David really know the kind of house God wanted?' Think about it – we wouldn't let any architect design a house for us without instructing them how we wanted it. Their building might be a good house, but it wouldn't be our house, would it? But the way God said 'no' to David's plan was even more wonderful than if he'd said 'yes'! This was his message for David:

> "The LORD declares to you that the LORD himself will establish a house for you: When your days are over and you rest with your fathers, I will raise up your offspring to succeed you, who will come from your own body, and I will establish his kingdom. He is the one who will build a house for my Name, and I will establish the throne of his kingdom for ever... Your house and your kingdom shall endure for ever before me: your throne shall be established forever'" (2 Samuel 7:11-13).

No doubt David was disappointed that his idea wouldn't see the light of day. His motivation was the purest, but even so, he was told he wasn't the man to do what he'd wanted to do for God. God had someone else in mind. However, as David thought about all that God had said in answer to him, he came to see that God's plans for him were even more wonderful than his plans for God. So his response to God was:

> *"Who am I, O Sovereign LORD, and what is my family, that you have brought me this far? And as if this were not enough in your sight, O Sovereign LORD, you have also spoken about the future of the house of your servant ... "How great you are, O Sovereign LORD! There is no-one like you ... "And now, LORD God, keep forever the promise you have made concerning your servant and his house... "O LORD Almighty, God of Israel, you have revealed this to your servant, saying, 'I will build a house for you'"* (2 Samuel 7:18-27).

We, too, can get over the disappointment of unfulfilled spiritual ambitions when we learn from our Bibles that God himself, and his plans for us, are far greater than we'd ever imagined before. So if we, like David, are trying to build a house for God today, not realizing that God has built his own, let's look again carefully at what God's said – and what he's not said – in his Word, for example through Paul in 1 Corinthians 3:11-15:

> *"No man can lay a foundation other than the one which is laid, which is Jesus Christ. Now if any man builds upon the foundation with gold, silver, precious stones, wood, hay, straw, each man's work will become evident;*

*for the day will show it, because it is to be revealed with
fire; and the fire itself will test the quality of each man's
work."*

If we have an idea of what should be foundational church
teaching – but it's different from God's revealed foundation –
the teaching the Lord taught his apostles as recorded in our
Bible – then we've still to discover that God's plan is far more
wonderful than our own

# CHAPTER 9 – FACING TEMPTATION

―――

How do you respond when you hear of a respected Christian who has committed a serious sin? Our next incident from the life of David illustrates the Bible warning: *'If you think you are standing firm, be careful that you don't fall!'* (1 Corinthians 10:12). In other words, it could happen to any of us. The whole point of considering this – and surely one of the reasons why we find it recorded in our Bibles – is to allow us to study the subtle workings of temptation, and see how one sin can lead to another. David's downward spiral deeper into sin began like this: *"In the spring, at the time when kings go off to war, David sent Joab out with the king's men and the whole Israelite army. They destroyed the Ammonites and besieged Rabbah. But David remained in Jerusalem"* (2 Samuel 11:1).

It must be important that the Bible author begins the story this way. It's significant that David's sin happened in the spring, which was the time when opposing forces tended to rejoin hostilities that'd been suspended for the winter. Whereas kings traditionally went out to war at this time, the author makes a definite point of saying that David remained behind in Jerusalem. The clear impression we get is this was David's first mistake. Here's the innocent-looking start of the downward spiral that would affect the course of the rest of David's life. Isn't there an expression that runs something like: 'The Devil will find something for idle hands to do'? David was indulging himself at home when: *"One evening he got up from his bed and walked around on the roof of the palace. From the roof he saw a woman bathing. The woman was very beautiful"* (2 Samuel 11:2).

There was nothing wrong with David walking round on the roof of his palace, as far as we know. A beautiful woman catches his eye. It's nothing more than an unintentional first glance. Still no problem. On the subject of tempting thoughts, and how to deal with them, Martin Luther once famously commented: 'We can't keep the birds from flying over our head, but we can keep them from building a nest in our hair!' Of course, he was comparing the birds to tempting thoughts. As David glanced Bathsheba's form, a thought flew into his mind. The problem built from there – the problem was what David did with this thought. He let it 'build a nest'. He was still in a mood to indulge himself. He: *"... sent someone to find out about her. The man said, "Isn't this Bathsheba, the daughter of Eliam and the wife of Uriah the Hittite?"* (2 Samuel 11:3)

At this point, now that he's found out the woman was married to one of his soldiers David should've dropped all further romantic thoughts about the woman. But, unfortunately, he'd already allowed the temptation to gain too much strength to be easily resisted. Finally: *"David sent messengers to get her. She came to him, and he slept with her ... Then she went back home. The woman conceived and sent word to David, saying, "I am pregnant"* (2 Samuel 11:4,5).

The apostle James in the New Testament helps us to understand the process by which temptation becomes sin. He says: *"Each one is tempted when he is carried away and enticed by his own* lust. *Then when lust has conceived, it gives birth to sin; and when sin is accomplished, it brings forth death*" (James 1:14-15). These words are a very apt summary of what happened here in the life of David. Temptation is usually easier to resist when it first confronts us. The longer we allow ourselves to be tempted, the weaker our defenses become. Eventually, we're so strongly under the spell of temptation that we've great difficulty resisting. Satan works at gradually eroding our defenses. He knows it's easier to get us to take a series of little steps than one big one. David's about to spiral down and down. In James' words, David's lustful thoughts have given birth to sin, and now it follows a deadly course of events, because:

> "*David sent ... word to Joab: "Send me Uriah the Hittite." And Joab sent him to David. When Uriah came to him, David asked him how Joab was, how the soldiers were and how the war was going. Then David said to Uriah, "Go down to your house ..." So Uriah left the palace, and a gift from the king was sent after him. But Uriah slept at the entrance to the palace with all his master's servants and did not go down to his house. When David was told, "Uriah did not go home," he asked him, "Haven't you just come from a distance? Why didn't you go home?" Uriah said to David, "The ark and Israel and Judah are staying in tents, and my master Joab and my lord's men are camped in the open fields. How could I go to my house to eat and drink and lie with my wife? As surely as you live, I will not do such a thing!"*

> *Then David said to him, "Stay here one more day, and tomorrow I will send you back." So Uriah remained in Jerusalem that day and the next. At David's invitation, he ate and drank with him, and David made him drunk. But in the evening Uriah went out to sleep on his mat among his master's servants; he did not go home. In the morning David wrote a letter to Joab and sent it with Uriah. In it he wrote, "Put Uriah in the front line where the fighting is fiercest. Then withdraw from him so that he will be struck down and die"* (2 Samuel 11:6-15).

Our sinful actions, like David's, can involve a number of other people. Here, obviously Bathsheba and Uriah are affected. David has wrecked their marriage, and effectively arranged Uriah's murder because he was too honorable, even in his innocence, to accommodate David's first attempt at cover up. David had hope he could fool everyone, including Uriah, that the child Bathsheba was expecting was Uriah's. But, in addition to Bathsheba and Uriah, Joab's integrity has been compromised, and several other soldiers fighting alongside Uriah were also killed when they were deliberately exposed to overwhelming odds. Tragically, none of this seemed to bother David so long as the message came back:

> *"Your servant Uriah the Hittite is dead." David told the messenger, "Say this to Joab: 'Don't let this upset you; the sword devours one as well as another. Press the attack against the city and destroy it.' Say this to encourage Joab." When Uriah's wife heard that her husband was*

*dead, she mourned for him. After the time of mourning*
*was over, David had her brought to his house, and she*
*became his wife and bore him a son. But the thing*
*David had done displeased the LORD"* (2 Samuel
11:24-27).

'Don't let this upset you!' How we trivialize sin! As we've
thought our sins often affect other people, but the most
important thing is that all sin is against God (Psalm 51:4). That's
why it's serious – and not only sexual sin, of course. David might
have thought he'd got away with it, but 'the thing David had
done displeased the LORD.' In the final analysis no-one gets
away with sin. A respected Christian, a church leader, the man
who thinks he's standing, yes, even the man after God's own
heart, can – and does – fall into temptation of different kinds.
It's not sin when we are tempted; it depends on how we respond
to that temptation. It's important to realize that we don't need
to fail. Paul tells us: *"No temptation has seized you expect what*
*is common to man. And God is faithful; he will not let you be*
*tempted beyond what you can bear. But when you are tempted, he*
*will also provide a way out so that you can stand up under it"* (1
Corinthians 10:13).

In temptation, we need to pray that we recognize the way of
escape and take it. But if we should fail, when we sin in any way,
it's so good to know in the words of the apostle John, that: *"the*
*blood of Jesus His Son cleanses us from all sin ... If we confess our*
*sins, He is faithful and righteous to forgive us our sins and to cleanse*
*us from all unrighteousness ... if anyone sins, we have an Advocate*
*with the Father, Jesus Christ the righteous"* (1 John 1:7–2:1).

To confess is far better than to cover up. As believers, we're assured we're saved forever from sin's penalty which Jesus bore for us on the cross; but it takes vigilance on our part day by day to work out our own salvation from sin's power so that our lives of service here are not made ineffective.

# CHAPTER 10 - GOD'S SEVERE MERCY

———

How do you tend to respond when someone confronts you about something you've done wrong? It's never comfortable, is it? Maybe because of that, if we've had to confront someone, we've chosen to go down an indirect route at first. That's what Nathan did when he confronted David with his sin. The sin in question was David's adultery with Bathsheba which he'd attempted to cover up by arranging her husband's death. Nathan's indirect approach when confronting David with this sin served a far more important purpose than simply helping him feel less awkward when challenging the king about his sinful behavior. If Nathan had confronted David directly, it's quite likely that David would have become defensive about his actions.

It's not clear whether Nathan was told by the Lord to handle the matter this way, or whether he was given the wisdom to decide for himself that this would be the most productive way to proceed. I'm sure he was fully aware that if he told David a story first and invited David to act as judge and jury so to speak, then David would tend to be more objective – and in doing so, would, of course, condemn himself. Now let's refresh our memory about what exactly happened ...

> "The LORD sent Nathan to David. When he came to him, he said, "There were two men in a certain town, one rich and the other poor. The rich man had a very

*large number of sheep and cattle, but the poor man had nothing except one little ewe lamb that he had bought. He raised it, and it grew up with him and his children. It shared his food, drank from his cup and even slept in his arms. It was like a daughter to him. Now a traveler came to the rich man, but the rich man refrained from taking one of his own sheep or cattle to prepare a meal for the traveler who had come to him. Instead, he took the ewe lamb that belonged to the poor man and prepared it for the one who had come to him"* (2 Samuel 12:1-4).

I think there was real skill displayed here in the fact Nathan chose to focus on the 'one little ewe lamb'. How could that fail to arouse sympathy from the king who'd been a shepherd boy committed to real care for his father's sheep? The tactic worked for:

*"David burned with anger against the man and said to Nathan, "As surely as the LORD lives, the man who did this deserves to die! He must pay for that lamb four times over, because he did such a thing and had no pity." Then Nathan said to David, "You are the man! This is what the LORD, the God of Israel, says: 'I anointed you king over Israel, and I delivered you from the hand of Saul. I gave your master's house to you, and your master's wives into your arms. I gave you the house of Israel and Judah. And if all this had been too little, I would have given you even more. Why did you despise the word of the LORD by doing what is evil in his eyes?*

*You struck down Uriah the Hittite with the sword and took his wife to be your own. You killed him with the sword of the Ammonites"* (2 Samuel 12:5-9).

The parallels were striking. David had everything he wanted – and more. But he repaid God's kindness by taking his neighbor's wife and committing murder in the cover-up. David was indeed the man who had shown no pity, and had despised the word of the LORD – had he not, in some sense, broken most, if not all, of the commands on the second (manward) table of the Law? But just as David in condemning the man in Nathan's story actually condemned himself, we can just as easily do the very same thing.

We express our disappointment that such a man as David should do such a thing, but what about ourselves? In some sense, might we not fit into Nathan's story too? God's given us every spiritual blessing in Christ (Ephesians 1:3) – he has lavished his love upon us (1 John 3:1) – but still we, like our Adam and Eve, can find ourselves setting our desire on some little forbidden pleasure. Even though David was the king, even though he'd found grace in God's sight, judgment was going to fall on him now, for God doesn't play favorites. Nathan now spells out to David the sentence God has imposed:

*"... the sword shall never depart from your house, because you despised me and took the wife of Uriah the Hittite to be your own.' ... Then David said to Nathan, "I have sinned against the LORD." Nathan replied, "The LORD has taken away your sin. You are not going*

*to die. But because by doing this you have made the enemies of the LORD show utter contempt, the son born to you will die"* (2 Samuel 12:10-14).

If that punishment seems severe to us, let's remember the penalty for adultery and murder should have been death on both counts under the Law. David had no right to live, but his life was spared. And whenever we read in the Bible of a judgment that seems severe, it should make us appreciate all the more what God did for us at the Cross – how severe was the punishment borne there by the Lord that he might be merciful to us for our sins! God's mercy is a severe mercy. It had to be paid for somewhere – and that place was the Cross of our Lord Jesus Christ.

*"On the seventh day the child died. David's servants were afraid to tell him that the child was dead, for they thought, "While the child was still living, we spoke to David but he would not listen to us. How can we tell him the child is dead? He may do something desperate." David noticed that his servants were whispering among themselves and he realized that the child was dead. "Is the child dead?" he asked. "Yes," they replied, "he is dead." Then David got up from the ground. After he had washed, put on lotions and changed his clothes, he went into the house of the LORD and worshipped. Then he went to his own house, and at his request they served him food, and he ate. His servants asked him, "Why are you acting in this way? While the child was alive, you fasted and wept, but now that the child is dead, you get up and eat!" He answered, "While the child was still*

*alive, I fasted and wept. I thought, 'Who knows? The LORD may be gracious to me and let the child live.' But now that he is dead, why should I fast? Can I bring him back again? I will go to him, but he will not return to me"* (2 Samuel 12:18-23).

These words have been a comfort to many who have known the terrible anguish of losing a child. For we can hold to the assurance David expressed here that his child – and any child now who dies before reaching the age of understanding – will automatically go into eternal blessing. And so: *"David comforted his wife Bathsheba and he went to her and lay with her. She gave birth to a son and they named him Solomon. The LORD loved him"* (2 Samuel 12:24).

Isn't it amazing – the man who in one sense ought never to have been born – Solomon – was the very one whom God loved and selected to build the temple instead of his father David. It seems like another token of God's severe mercy. We thank God that he's indeed merciful to sinners who through his grace turn to him for forgiveness. David certainly did. It doesn't take a great man to commit a great sin, but something of David's greatness is shown by his response. Psalm 51 captures his broken spirit:

*"Have mercy on me, O God, according to your unfailing love; according to your great compassion blot out my transgressions. Wash away all my iniquity and cleanse me from my sin ... Against you, you only, have I sinned and done what is evil in your sight ... Surely I was sinful at birth, sinful from the time my mother conceived me"* (Psalm 51:1-10).

It's here – in confession – that we leave David, taking away for ourselves a reminder of the great promise made with us through the apostle John, that: *"If we confess our sins, He is faithful and righteous to forgive us our sins and to cleanse us from all unrighteousness"* (1 John 1:9). And the other reminder from the apostle Paul in Galatians 6, if we are confronting sin in someone else, that: *"If a man is caught in any trespass, you who are spiritual restore such a one in a spirit of gentleness; each one looking to yourself, lest you too be tempted"* (Galatians 6:1).

# CHAPTER 11 – MISPLACED TRUST

———

Now we come to another of those very dramatic episodes in the life of David that provides us with a highly relevant lesson. At first, the difference in circumstances between ourselves and David might give us the mistaken impression that there's nothing directly relevant for us here. But I hope that a moment's reflection will convince us that there's something here that's relevant to every follower of the Lord Jesus Christ. Sometimes the experiences we pass through put us to the test of discovering what it really is in practice that we're putting our trust in. Of course, we'd all say that our trust is in the Lord. But to some extent things like a steady job and a large savings account balance will tend to contribute to our feelings of security.

Obviously, there's nothing inherently wrong with these things. If our focus remains on God as the giver of all good gifts, then our trust in him will be unaffected. But it's when we drift into putting our trust in the gifts themselves – rather than the Giver – it's then that we reach the stage when our trust has become misplaced. So our look into the life of David is intended to teach us that our trust must always be in the Lord and not in our human strength or resources. Here's the way in which David faced the challenge:

> "Satan rose up against Israel and incited David to take a census of Israel. So David said to Joab and the commanders of the troops "Go and count the Israelites from Beersheba to Dan. Then report back to me so that I may know how many there are." But Joab replied, "May the LORD multiply his troops a hundred times over. My lord the king, are they not all my lord's subjects? Why does my lord want to do this? Why should he bring guilt on Israel?" The king's word, however, overruled Joab; so Joab left and went throughout Israel and then came back to Jerusalem. Joab reported the number of the fighting men to David: in all Israel there were one million one hundred thousand men who could handle a sword, including four hundred and seventy thousand in Judah. But Joab did not include Levi and Benjamin in the numbering, because the king's command was repulsive to him. This command was also evil in the sight of God; so he punished Israel" (1 Chronicles 21:1-7).

The Bible could hardly have made it any clearer that what David had done was wrong. We're told it was the result of Satan inciting him to do something which was evil in the sight of God. Even David's general, the man called Joab, realized very clearly that this was a wrong action which could only end up bringing guilt on Israel. His objection, however, was overruled and under pressure he performed the census David ordered. Even so, he did his best to reduce the number that was given back to David. On the surface, it may have seemed to us that this was no big deal. But the mention of Satanic involvement and God's displeasure at David's action surely has the effect of capturing our attention – and alerting us to the fact that there's a serious issue behind all this. It's seems likely that David was motivated by sinful pride in ordering this census, and that he was placing his trust at that moment in the size of his army rather than in God.

This is a strong temptation in our culture too. For, are we not encouraged to put our trust in our abilities, our experience, our level of education, or any number of visible, tangible things? But we need to learn, like David, that many of these things can be taken away in a moment. We need to learn, and sometimes relearn, that the only lasting security is in the Lord.

> "Then David said to God, "I have sinned greatly by doing this. Now, I beg you take away the guilt of your servant. I have done a very foolish thing." The LORD said to Gad, David's seer, "Go and tell David, 'This is what the LORD says: I am giving you three options. Choose one of them for me to carry out against you.'" So Gad went to David and said to him, "This is what the LORD says: 'Take your choice: three years of famine, three months of being swept away before your enemies, with their swords overtaking you, or three days of the sword of the LORD – days of plague in the land, with the angel of the LORD ravaging every part of Israel.'
>
> Now then, decide how I should answer the one who sent me." David said to Gad, "I am in deep distress. Let me fall into the hands of the LORD, for his mercy is very great; but do not let me fall into the hands of men." So the LORD sent a plague on Israel, and seventy thousand

> *men of Israel fell dead. And God sent an angel to destroy*
> *Jerusalem. But as the angel was doing so, the LORD*
> *saw it and was grieved because of the calamity and said*
> *to the angel who was destroying the people, "Enough!*
> *Withdraw your hand." The angel of the LORD was then*
> *standing at the threshing-floor of Araunah the Jebusite"*
> (1 Chronicles 21:8-15).

I wonder if the thought crossed David's mind that 70,000 men in Israel had fallen in three days – surely a higher death toll than in most battles. Remember, David had probably numbered his army so as to feel secure against attack. We might think it harsh that so many should die when it was David who sinned, but elsewhere the Bible (2 Samuel 24:1) tells us that God was angry with Israel at this time, not just with David. So this was a wider punishment as well, and we need to bear that in mind. Curiously, at first, we find the Bible paying a lot of attention to the place where the plague stopped – in fact, about half a chapter is devoted to it. This appears to be for the purpose of explaining to us how the site for the new temple was acquired, for:

> *"... the angel of the LORD ordered Gad to tell David*
> *to go up and build an altar to the LORD on the*
> *threshing-floor of Araunah the Jebusite ... Araunah said*
> *to David, "Take it! Let my lord the king do whatever*
> *pleases him. Look, I will give the oxen for the burnt*
> *offerings, the threshing-sledges for the wood, and the*
> *wheat for the grain offering. I will give all this." But*
> *King David replied to Araunah, "No, I insist on paying*
> *the full price. I will not take for the LORD what is*

*yours, or sacrifice a burnt offering that costs me nothing."*
*So David paid Araunah six hundred shekels of gold for*
*the site. David built an altar to the LORD there and*
*sacrificed burnt offerings and fellowship offerings. He*
*called on the LORD, and the LORD answered him*
*with fire from heaven on the altar of burnt offering ...*
*Then David said, "The house of the LORD God is to be*
*here, and also the altar of burnt offering for Israel"* (1
Chronicles 21:18–22:1).

The temple was to be built in the place where God's anger was satisfied, in the place where the sin of God's people was dealt with, the place of costly sacrifice. It would also be intimately associated with this lesson of having our trust fully and obediently in the Lord himself and in his Word. All of which brings us to the further application: 'Does God have a holy temple on earth today?' Yes, is the resounding answer of the New Testament. Not made with human hands, of course, Stephen the first recorded Christian martyr made that clear at the beginning of Christian history (Acts 7:48). Peter, writing later in the Bible, adds to our understanding when he tells us God's spiritual temple in the present age is made of living stones (1 Peter 2:5) – stones quarried at Calvary – and built together on the one and only foundation, the teaching of the Christ of the Cross.

God's choice for this entire age is that the Lord's teaching, which became known as 'the apostles teaching', should be the basis for his house or dwelling-place on earth. If our trust, expressed in ongoing obedience, is placed in the word of the cross in all its fullness (e.g. see Acts 2:41,42); then forgiven and faithful, we, too, will discover the place of God's house today.

# CHAPTER 12 – GENEROUS GIVING

———

I recently visited an elderly lady who was living on her own and receiving a pension as her means of support. She was showing me her mail from the last week. It was a shopping-bagful of what were mainly appeals for money from a whole range of charities, especially those caring for animals and children. This dear old lady was very tender-hearted and found it impossible to resist letters bearing photographs of mal-nourished dogs etc. You'll realize she was an animal-lover. I was shocked when she told me she regularly donated more than her entire pension each month.

I don't know how you respond to appeals for money. Like me, you may receive many appeals for financial support, many of them from worthy causes. Some wisdom is required, for we can hardly give to them all (Romans 16:19). As Christians we'd surely want to find out the Lord's will in this matter of giving, as in all other matters. We need to be wise in the use of the resources the Lord has entrusted us with. Of course, we can find direct guidance on this practical matter in the New Testament of our Bible. But many of the main points taught there are illustrated for us in the life of David. This, then, will be the focus of our concluding chapter, for in it we'll see how David gave generously and joyously to the Lord.

As recorded in 1 Chronicles 29:1-30, David graciously acknowledged that God had chosen his son Solomon, and not himself, to build the temple at Jerusalem, even though it'd been David's own strong desire to build it. Not grudgingly, but generously, David set about assisting Solomon's future work of building. In his own words, he realized that:

> "The task is great, because this palatial structure is not for man but for the LORD God. With all my resources I have provided for the temple of my God – gold for the gold work, silver for the silver, bronze for the bronze, iron for the iron and wood for the wood, as well as onyx for the settings, turquoise, stones of various colors, and all kinds of fine stone and marble – all of these in large quantities. Besides, in my devotion to the temple of my God I now give my personal treasures of gold and silver for the temple of my God, over and above everything I have provided for this holy temple" (1 Chronicles 29:1-3).

Notice that when David spoke about providing his 'personal treasures' and his 'resources', it was in the same breath as when he spoke of his 'devotion' toward God and the temple-building project. This demonstrates the attitude that motivated David's giving. God's more interested in the attitude of our heart as we give than in the actual amount we give. As the apostle Paul says in 2 Corinthians 8:12: "... if the readiness is present, it is acceptable according to what a man has, not according to what he does not have."

But it's staggering, all the same, to think that David gave literally tons of gold and silver. His inspiring example encouraged others to give handsomely as well. And their example encourages us, too, - and all in a way that agrees with the New Testament's teaching when it says: *"he who sows sparingly shall also reap sparingly; and he who sows bountifully shall also reap bountifully"* (2 Corinthians 9:6). That's dealing with our financial giving to the Lord – to the work of the Lord – using the analogy of the farmer giving out his seed. The more seed he sows, the better the harvest. God no longer prescribes the tithe, or tenth, for Christian giving. Like David, we too can give 'over and above', but each one is to: *"put aside and save, as he may prosper"* (1 Corinthians 16:2).

If you look at these words of Paul in their context at the beginning of First Corinthians chapter 16, you'll see they underline that our giving should be the subject of advance planning. Our 'leftovers' and our 'surplus' are not worthy of God. But let's return to the point we were making about how David's inspiring example encouraged others to give handsomely as well. This is what we read:

> *"The people rejoiced at the willing response of their leaders, for they had given freely and wholeheartedly to the LORD. David the king also rejoiced greatly. David praised the LORD in the presence of the whole assembly, saying, "Praise be to you, O LORD, God of our father Israel, from everlasting to everlasting. Yours, O LORD, is the greatness and the power and the glory and the majesty and the splendor, for everything in heaven and earth is yours. Yours, O LORD, is the kingdom; you*

*are exalted as head over all. Wealth and honor come
from you; you are the ruler of all things. In your hands
are strength and power to exalt and give strength to
all. Now, our God, we give you thanks, and praise your
glorious name"* (1 Chronicles 29:9-13).

There's a danger that we can boast about our giving. Celebrities
milk the publicity value of charitable giving. The Lord Jesus
denounced as hypocrites the religious leaders of his day who
sounded trumpets when they gave to the poor (Matthew 6:2).
The Lord said that public recognition was all the reward they'd
get. David's attitude here is refreshingly different. What a high
view of God he expresses! David's boasting is in God as the
ultimate giver of all, and not in his own giving to God in return.
David acknowledges that all he's been able to give has come from
God in the first place. He says:

*"Who am I, and who are my people, that we should
be able to give as generously as this? Everything comes
from you, and we have given you only what comes from
your hand. We are aliens and strangers in your sight,
as were all forefathers. Our days on earth are like a
shadow, without hope. O LORD our God, as for all this
abundance that we have provided for building you a
temple for your Holy Name, it comes from your hand
and all of it belongs to you. I know, my God, that you
test the heart and are pleased with integrity. All these
things have I given willingly and with honest intent.
And now I have seen with joy how willingly your people
who are here have given to you. O LORD, God of our*

*fathers Abraham, Isaac and Israel, keep this desire in the
hearts of your people forever, and keep their hearts loyal
to you"* (1 Chronicles 29:14-18).

David saw giving as a matter of the heart – something to be done
with integrity. Above all he emphasizes the aspect of willing
and joyful giving. This illustrates the direct teaching later given
through the apostle Paul: *"Let each one do just as he has purposed
in his heart; not grudgingly or under compulsion; for God loves a
cheerful give"* (2 Corinthians 9:7).

David realized the Lord was the source of all his wealth, and
so he was generous in his giving back to God. Because he
recognized that God already owns everything, he saw there was
no reason to boast in the amount he'd been enabled to give.
David's appreciation of God seems to go hand in hand with his
willingness to give. In our case too, surely our willingness, or
unwillingness, to give will reflect accurately our appreciation of
God. When we, like David, grasp the greatness of God, we'll
be motivated to worship him through our financial giving too
(Philippians 4:18).

It's fitting then that our look at the life of David concludes with
a look at his generous giving. To underline the challenge of his
generosity to our hearts, I want to remind you in closing that
in Second Corinthians chapter 9 to which we've referred – the
older Bible versions actually use two different words to express
the idea of generosity. They are 'bountifully' (or 'bounty') as well
as 'liberally' (or 'with all liberality'). In some versions at least,
the giving of the Corinthians is spoken of as their 'bounty' (in
verse 5). That literally means a 'spoken benediction'. It reminds us

that what we give is more than what it's worth in purely financial terms, it's a token of our conferred goodwill – it's an expression of love.

The other word, liberality, has the idea of 'singleness'. At first the idea of singleness seems totally unrelated to the business of giving. But Jesus taught that no-one can serve two masters: and certainly not God and money. 'Singleness' in this sense means freedom from the double-mindedness that would taint our giving with selfish motivation. When we give 'with singleness' we're not looking for a pay-off ourselves – and as we've seen already, that was the way David gave to God.

# CHAPTER 13 – STUDY GUIDE

———

## 1. God looks at the heart - Reference: 1 Samuel 16:1-13

a. In these days of 'PR' & 'spin', image is everything. How might Saul have appeared to be the ideal candidate by worldly standards of leadership?

b. What sort of 'outward things' (v.7) do we tend to look for in people, and how does our culture tend to reinforce this?

c. Why do you think God got Samuel to look at each of Jesse's sons before revealing that he had chosen David?

d. What 'inner qualities' does God value; and how can we develop them?

## 2. The Battle is the Lord's - Reference: 1 Samuel 17

a. When you're faced with a challenge seemingly beyond your abilities, how do you tend to respond?

b. One of the myths of our culture is 'if you set your mind to it, you can do anything'. How is this myth confronted here?

c. What had the Israelites forgotten about God's promises (see Deut.20:1-4)

d. What biblical promises do we need to remember during the battles of life?

e. Are human qualifications irrelevant (see Zech.4:6)?

## 3. True Friendship - Reference: 1 Samuel 18:1-4; 20:1-17, 30-42; 2 Samuel 1:25-27

a. What qualities do you appreciate most in a friend, and why?

b. What commitment did they take make to each other, and what kinds of mutual commitments can strengthen our friendships?

c. What did Jonathan's friendship cost him? In what (other) ways can friendship be costly?

d. What impresses you most about Jonathan & David's friendship?

## 4. A Matter of Conscience - Reference: 1 Samuel 24

a. In finding God's will, we often take account of circumstances and opportunities, which might have convinced David he should kill Saul?

b. What additional factors convinced David he shouldn't mistreat Saul?

c. When, if ever, is it right to go against our conscience?

d. Jacob was someone who tried to make things happen, David left the outworking of promises to God. The result appears to be the same – what's the difference? Is it ever right to take matters into our own hands?

## 5. Secure in the Lord - Reference: 1 Samuel 25

a. Someone once dumped a large load of rubbish on a man's private property. The man found the offender's name amid the mess, and so returned all the rubbish to the sender's front garden. Do you think this was justified?

b. What methods do we sometimes used to 'get even' with those who mistreat us?

c. David's intended action against Nabal is sandwiched between two accounts of his sparing Saul's life. What do you make of this context?

d. What impresses you about Abigail's response; and what was the Lord telling David?

## 6. Finding Strength in the Lord - Reference: 1 Samuel 30:1-25

a. The Christian life is often portrayed as a before-and-after story (everything after conversion being perfectly good). What do you think about that?

b. How have you reacted when you felt overwhelmed by a problem?

c. How did David (v.6) and how can we, find strength in such circumstances?

d. How does v.23 help us to have a balanced view of why God allows difficulties to come into our lives?

## 7. God's Wrath & Blessing - Reference: 2 Samuel 6

a. Why do you think David and the people viewed this as an occasion to celebrate with all their might?

b. If Uzzah's act was well-intentioned, why did the Lord smite him?

c. Why is there contrasting blessing in vv. 10-11?

d. How does this chapter help us to understand how we're to serve God?

## 8. Unfulfilled Wishes - Reference: 2 Samuel 7

a. Have you ever wanted to do something for God which hasn't prospered?

b. What had David and Nathan both failed to take account of (v.7)?

c. How might we attempt to build something for God which he's not asked for?

d. How did God's plans for David turn out to be better than David's plans for God?

## 9. Facing Temptation - Reference: 2 Samuel 11

a. How do you respond when you hear that a respected Christian has committed a serious sin?

b At what point does a temptation become sin?

c. Why do we, like David, prefer cover-ups to confession?

d. What led a 'man after God's own heart' to commit adultery & murder, and how can it be a warning to us?

## 10. God's Severe Mercy - Reference: 2 Samuel 12

a. How do you tend to respond when someone confronts you about something you know you've done wrong?

b. Why did Nathan use the indirect device of telling a story?

c. In what way do we display contempt for God and his Word when we sin (v.9)?

d. How is God's justice and mercy seen in his decision about David's sin?

## 11. Misplaced Trust - Reference: 1 Chronicles 21:1 – 22:1

a. What sort of things contribute to your feelings of security?

b. Why was David's action in numbering the people sinful?

c. Why are we often tempted to trust in human strength and resources rather than in the Lord?

d. Why does the author devote so much space to David's purchase of the threshing floor; and why this site for the temple?

## 12. Generous Giving - Reference: 1 Chronicles 29

a. How do you respond to appeals for money?

b What New Testament principles for our giving are illustrated here?

c. Expand on David's view of God (vv.10-13).

d. Does our (un)willingness to give to God reflect our view of him?

Did you love *After God's Own Heart : The Life of David*? Then you should read *Abraham: Friend of God* by Brian Johnston!

Bible teacher, missionary and radio broadcaster, Brian Johnston's conversational and down to earth approach provides an informative biography and commentary of one of the most important characters in the Old Testament of our Bibles – Abraham the nomad. Abraham was known for his great example of faith and for being a "Friend of God", but his life was far from plain sailing. Brian draws out a number of lessons for our discipleship today in this helpful Bible study.

# Also by Brian Johnston

Healthy Churches - God's Bible Blueprint For Growth
Hope for Humanity: God's Fix for a Broken World
First Corinthians: Nothing But Christ Crucified
Bible Answers to Listeners' Questions
Living in God's House: His Design in Action
Christianity 101: Seven Bible Basics
Nights of Old: Bible Stories of God at Work
Daniel Decoded: Deciphering Bible Prophecy
A Test of Commitment: 15 Challenges to Stimulate Your
Devotion to Christ
John's Epistles - Certainty in the Face of Change
If Atheism Is True...
8 Amazing Privileges of God's People: A Bible Study of Romans
9:4-5
Learning from Bible Grandparents
Increasing Your Christian Footprint
Christ-centred Faith
Mindfulness That Jesus Endorses
Amazing Grace! Paul's Gospel Message to the Galatians
Abraham: Friend of God
The Future in Bible Prophecy
Unlocking Hebrews
Learning How To Pray - From the Lord's Prayer

About the Bush: The Five Excuses of Moses
The Five Loves of God
Deepening Our Relationship With Christ
Really Good News For Today!
A Legacy of Kings - Israel's Chequered History
Minor Prophets: Major Issues!
The Tabernacle - God's House of Shadows
Tribes and Tribulations - Israel's Predicted Personalities
Once Saved, Always Saved - The Reality of Eternal Security
After God's Own Heart : The Life of David
Jesus: What Does the Bible Really Say?
God: His Glory, His Building, His Son
The Feasts of Jehovah in One Hour
Knowing God - Reflections on Psalm 23
Praying with Paul
Get Real ... Living Every Day as an Authentic Follower of
Christ
A Crisis of Identity
Double Vision: Hidden Meanings in the Prophecy of Isaiah
Samson: A Type of Christ
Great Spiritual Movements
Take Your Mark's Gospel
Total Conviction - 4 Things God Wants You To Be Fully
Convinced About
Esther: A Date With Destiny
Experiencing God in Ephesians
James - Epistle of Straw?
The Supremacy of Christ
The Visions of Zechariah
Encounters at the Cross
Five Sacred Solos - The Truths That the Reformation Recovered

Kingdom of God: Past, Present or Future?
Overcoming Objections to Christian Faith
Stronger Than the Storm - The Last Words of Jesus
Fencepost Turtles - People Placed by God
Five Woman and a Baby - The Genealogy of Jesus
Pure Milk - Nurturing New Life in Jesus
Jesus: Son Over God's House
Salt and the Sacrifice of Christ
The Glory of God
The Way: Being a New Testament Disciple
Power Outage - Christianity Unplugged
Windows to Faith: Insights for the Inquisitive
Home Truths
60 Minutes to Raise the Dead

# About the Author

Born and educated in Scotland, Brian worked as a government scientist until God called him into full-time Christian ministry on behalf of the Churches of God (www.churchesofgod.info). His voice has been heard on Search For Truth radio broadcasts for over 30 years (visit www.searchfortruth.podbean.com) during which time he has been an itinerant Bible teacher throughout the UK and Canada. His evangelical and missionary work outside the UK is primarily in Belgium and The Philippines. He is married to Rosemary, with a son and daughter.

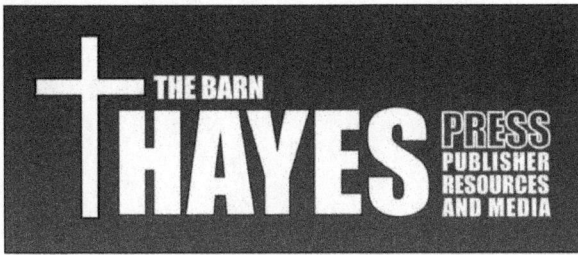

# About the Publisher

Hayes Press (www.hayespress.org) is a registered charity in the United Kingdom, whose primary mission is to disseminate the Word of God, mainly through literature. It is one of the largest distributors of gospel tracts and leaflets in the United Kingdom, with over 100 titles and hundreds of thousands despatched annually. In addition to paperbacks and eBooks, Hayes Press also publishes Plus Eagles Wings, a fun and educational Bible magazine for children, and Golden Bells, a popular daily Bible reading calendar in wall or desk formats. Also available are over 100 Bibles in many different versions, shapes and sizes, Bible text posters and much more!

www.ingramcontent.com/pod-product-compliance
Lightning Source LLC
Chambersburg PA
CBHW021210020426
42331CB00003B/295